LEISURE ARTS, INC. • Maumelle, Arkansas

YOU NEED THIS

- ❏ 4 ounces (or ½ cup) white glue
- ❏ ½ cup water
- ❏ ½ cup liquid starch
- ❏ Desired color liquid food coloring

This recipe can be doubled.
We mixed up a double batch.

SIMPLE SLIME

Start with this simple recipe to really get a feel for making slime. Each of the other slime recipes list exactly what you need to make that particular type of slime. All slime recipes contain glue (white or clear school or general purpose glue) and an activator (liquid starch, which is available near the laundry detergent).

READ THIS!

→ Store your slime for about a week in a covered, air-tight container. After that, place in a resealable plastic bag and throw away. Do not pour down the drain or flush down the toilet.

→ Slime is not edible; do not eat, ingest, or place in mouth or nose.

→ Slime is not for children under 8 years old. Keep away from small children & pets. Colored slime may stain clothing & furniture. Adult supervision recommended. Extended use not recommended.

DO THIS

1. Pour the glue and the water into a large bowl. Gently stir until the two are thoroughly mixed together. Scrape the sides as needed.

2. Add the food coloring, starting with about 10 drops. If you'd like a darker color, add more food coloring, about 5 drops at a time. Liquid food coloring will not get intensely dark, no matter how much you add.

3. Shake the starch well before you measure it out. Pour the starch into the glue mixture. Gently stir, scraping the sides as needed. The mixture will start to thicken and form slime. Keep stirring until most, if not all, of the liquid is absorbed.

4. Knead the slime with both hands in the bowl until it starts to come together into a soft lump or ball. Place the slime on the table and knead some more. Continue kneading until the slime is stretchy and no longer sticky.

5. Clean-up is easy; just wash the spatula, bowl, and measuring cup with hot soapy water. Store the slime for about a week in an airtight container.

CLEAR

YOU NEED THIS
- ☐ 4 ounces (or ½ cup) clear glue
- ☐ ½ cup water
- ☐ ¼-½ cup liquid starch

DO THIS

1. Pour the glue and water into a large bowl. Gently stir until the two are thoroughly mixed together. Scrape the sides as needed.

2. Shake the starch well before you measure it out. Add a small amount of the liquid starch to the glue mixture and gently stir. The mixture will start to thicken and form slime. Keep stirring until the starch is well combined into the glue mixture.

3. Add a bit more liquid starch and stir very well. You may or may not need to add more starch. Add just enough to bring the slime into a soft lump or a ball. Adding too much of the starch will cause the slime to get very firm and not slime-like.

4. Knead the slime with both hands in the bowl for a bit. Place it on the table and knead some more. Continue kneading until the slime is stretchy and no longer sticky. The slime will be full of air bubble and won't be clear, but that is OK.

5. Place the slime into an airtight container and do not disturb it for at least 3 days. The air bubbles will settle.

6. Clean-up is easy; just wash the spatula, bowl, and measuring cup with hot soapy water.

TIP

We used a borax mixture as the activator (instead of liquid starch) to make our slime even more transparent. Mix 1 tsp borax in 1 cup warm water. After mixing the glue and water together, add 3 tsp of the borax mixture. Stir as directed and add more borax mixture, 1 tsp at a time, until the slime comes together. Continue with Steps 4-6.

7

GLITTER GLUE

YOU NEED THIS
- ☐ 6 ounce bottle glitter glue
- ☐ 3 Tbsps water
- ☐ ¼-½ cup liquid starch

DO THIS

1. Pour the glue into a large bowl. Add water and stir until thoroughly mixed together.

2. Shake the starch well before you measure it out. Add a small amount of the liquid starch to the glue mixture and gently stir. The mixture will start to thicken and form slime. Keep stirring until the starch is well combined into the glue mixture.

3. Add a bit more liquid starch and stir very well. You may or may not need to add more starch. Add just enough to bring the slime into a soft lump or a ball. Adding too much of the starch will cause the slime to get very firm and not slime-like.

4. Knead the slime with both hands in the bowl for a bit. Place it on the table and knead some more. Continue kneading until the slime is stretchy and no longer sticky.

5. Clean-up is easy; just wash the spatula, bowl, measuring spoon, and measuring cup with hot soapy water. Store the slime for about a week in an airtight container.

TIP

For a more transparent slime, try substituting 1 tsp borax mixed into 1 cup warm water for the starch. Start off by adding 3 tsp of the borax mixture. Continue as in Steps 3-5, adding the borax mixture 1 tsp at a time, to achieve slime.

YOU NEED THIS
- ☐ 5 ounce bottle clear glue
- ☐ 2 Tbsps metallic gold acrylic paint
- ☐ ¼ cup liquid starch

DO THIS

This recipe can be doubled.

1. Pour the glue into a large bowl. Add the gold paint and stir until thoroughly mixed together.

2. Shake the starch well before you measure it out. Add a small amount of the liquid starch to the glue mixture and gently stir. The mixture will start to thicken and form slime. Keep stirring until the starch is well combined into the glue mixture.

3. Add a bit more liquid starch and stir very well. You may or may not need to add more starch. Add just enough to bring the slime into a soft lump or a ball. Adding too much of the starch will cause the slime to get very firm and not slime-like.

4. Knead the slime with both hands in the bowl for a bit. Place it on the table and knead some more. Continue kneading until the slime is stretchy and no longer sticky.

5. Clean-up is easy; just wash the spatula, bowl, measuring spoon, and measuring cup with hot soapy water. Store the slime for about a week in an airtight container.

MAGNETIC

YOU NEED THIS

- ¼ cup white glue
- 2 Tbsps synthetic black iron oxide – Fe3O4 (available online)
- ¼ cup liquid starch
- very strong, rare earth magnet (we used a ½" x ½" x 4" neodymium magnet)
- disposable gloves

DO THIS

1. Pour the glue into a large bowl. Add the iron oxide and stir until thoroughly mixed together.

2. Shake the starch well before you measure it out. Add a small amount of the liquid starch to the glue mixture and gently stir. The mixture will start to thicken and form slime. Keep stirring until the starch is well combined into the glue mixture.

3. Add a bit more liquid starch and stir very well. You may or may not need to add more starch. Add just enough to bring the slime into a soft lump or a ball. Adding too much of the starch will cause the slime to get very firm and not slime-like.

4. Wearing gloves, knead the slime with both hands in the bowl for a bit. Place it on a covered work surface and knead some more. Continue kneading until the slime is stretchy and no longer sticky.

5. Clean-up is easy; just wash the spatula, bowl, measuring spoon, and measuring cup with hot soapy water. Store the slime for about a week in an airtight container.

READ THIS!

Be careful not to breathe in the iron oxide powder. Have an adult measure & add it to the glue for you.

Neodymium magnets are extremely strong! Keep them away from cell phones, computers, & other electronics. Keep all magnets away from small children & pets. If your magnet gets stuck to an object, slide the magnet & the object apart; do not try to pull them apart.

COLOR CHANGING

YOU NEED THIS

- ☐ ¼ cup white glue
- ☐ 1 Tbsp water
- ☐ 3 tsps thermochromatic pigment (available online)
- ☐ liquid food coloring (see TIP below)
- ☐ ⅛ cup liquid starch

DO THIS

1. Pour the glue into a large bowl. Add the water and stir until thoroughly mixed together. Add 5 drops of food coloring and stir until thoroughly blended.

2. Add the pigment to the glue mixture and gently stir. Keep stirring until the pigment is completely combined with the glue mixture.

3. Shake the starch well before you measure it out. Add a small amount of the liquid starch to the glue mixture and gently stir. The mixture will start to thicken and form slime. Keep stirring until the starch is well combined into the glue mixture.

4. Add a bit more liquid starch and stir very well. You may or may not need to add more starch. Add just enough to bring the slime into a soft lump or a ball. Adding too much of the starch will cause the slime to get very firm and not slime-like.

5. Knead the slime with both hands in the bowl for a bit. Place it on the table and knead some more. Continue kneading until the slime is stretchy and no longer sticky.

6. Clean-up is easy; just wash the spatula, bowl, measuring spoons, and measuring cup with hot soapy water. Store the slime for about a week in an airtight container.

TIP

Thermochromatic pigment is available in several colors & reactive temperature ranges. The pigments will change color with the application of heat. Some pigments will go clear when warmed; others will actually change color. Also, some pigments will change at temperatures just above room temperature, making them easy to change with the warmth of your hands. Choose a contrasting color of food coloring for the clear reactive pigments.

14   www.leisurearts.com

STARRY NIGHT

YOU NEED THIS

- ☐ 4 ounces (or ½ cup) white glue
- ☐ ½ cup water
- ☐ ½ cup liquid starch
- ☐ black paste food coloring
- ☐ neon yellow fine glitter
- ☐ silver fine glitter
- ☐ holographic/iridescent glitter
- ☐ silver star sequins
- ☐ toothpick or disposable plastic fork

DO THIS

1. Pour the glue and the water into a large bowl. Gently stir until the two are thoroughly mixed together. Scrape the sides as needed.

2. Add a small amount of food coloring by dipping a toothpick or the tines of a disposable fork into the paste and adding it to the glue mixture. Stir it in. Continue to add paste coloring until you achieve the desired color. *Note: This paste food coloring should now be dedicated to craft projects only, no cake, cookie, or other baking recipes!*

3. Add the yellow glitter, silver glitter, and holographic glitter, mixing thoroughly into the glue mixture. Mix in as much glitter as you like. Mix in the silver star sequins, adding as many as desired.

4. Shake the starch well before you measure it out. Pour the starch into the glue mixture. Gently stir, scraping the sides as needed. The mixture will start to thicken and form slime. Keep stirring until most, if not all, of the liquid is absorbed.

5. Knead the slime with both hands in the bowl until it starts to come together into a soft lump. Place it on a covered work surface and knead some more. Continue kneading until the slime is stretchy and no longer sticky.

6. Clean-up is easy; just wash the spatula, bowl, and measuring cup with hot soapy water. Store the slime for about a week in an airtight container.

GLITTER

YOU NEED THIS

- ☐ 2 5 ounce bottles clear glue
- ☐ 1/2 cup water
- ☐ glitter (We used a multi-color chunky glitter.)
- ☐ 1/4-1/2 cup liquid starch

DO THIS

1. Pour the glue and water into a large bowl. Gently stir until the two are thoroughly mixed together. Scrape the sides as needed.

2. Add the glitter and stir until it is thoroughly mixed in.

3. Shake the starch well before you measure it out. Add a small amount of the liquid starch to the glue mixture and gently stir. The mixture will start to thicken and form slime. Keep stirring until the starch is well combined into the glue mixture.

4. Add a bit more liquid starch and stir very well. You may or may not need to add more starch. Add just enough to bring the slime into a soft lump or a ball. Adding too much of the starch will cause the slime to get very firm and not slime-like.

5. Knead the slime with both hands in the bowl for a bit. Place it on the table and knead some more. Continue kneading until the slime is stretchy and no longer sticky.

6. Clean-up is easy; just wash the spatula, bowl, and measuring cup with hot soapy water. Store the slime for about a week in an airtight container.

TIP

For a more transparent slime, try substituting 1 tsp borax mixed into 1 cup warm water for the starch. Start off by adding 3 tsp of the borax mixture. Continue as in Steps 3-6, adding the borax mixture 1 tsp at a time, to achieve slime.

FLUFFY

YOU NEED THIS

- ☐ 1/2 cup white glue
- ☐ 1/2 cup shaving cream
- ☐ 1/2 cup foaming hand soap
- ☐ 1 Tbsp plus 1 tsp cornstarch
- ☐ 6-7 pumps of regular liquid hand soap in pump dispenser
- ☐ 6-7 pumps of hand lotion in pump dispenser
- ☐ desired color liquid food coloring
- ☐ 1/4-1/2 cup liquid starch

DO THIS

This recipe can be doubled.

1. Mix the glue, shaving cream, and foaming hand soap in a large bowl. Gently stir in the cornstarch. Scrape the sides as needed.

2. Mix in the liquid hand soap and hand lotion. Add the food coloring, starting with about 10 drops. If you'd like a darker color, add more food coloring, about 5 drops at a time.

3.Shake the starch well before you measure it out. Add a small amount of the liquid starch to the glue mixture and gently stir. The mixture will start to thicken and form slime. Keep stirring until the starch is well combined into the glue mixture.

4. Add a bit more liquid starch and stir very well. You may or may not need to add more starch. Add just enough to bring the slime into a soft lump or a ball. Adding too much of the starch will cause the slime to get very firm and not slime-like.

5. Knead the slime with both hands in the bowl. Place it on the table and knead some more. Continue kneading until the slime is stretchy and no longer sticky. If the slime is not stretchy, add 3 pumps of hand lotion. This really helps the stretch factor. Keep adding lotion until slime is as stretchy as you'd like.

6. Clean-up is easy; just wash the spatula, bowl, measuring spoons, and measuring cup with hot soapy water. Store the slime for about a week in an airtight container.

TIP

This light, fluffy slime can have any scent you choose. Just pick shaving cream, hand soaps, & lotion that have complementary scents.

WINTER

YOU NEED THIS

- ☐ 4 ounces (or ½ cup) white glue
- ☐ 2½ Tbsps water
- ☐ ¼-½ cup liquid starch
- ☐ ⅓ cup polystyrene mini beads
- ☐ silver fine glitter
- ☐ white iridescent snowflake sequins
- ☐ blue food coloring

DO THIS

1. Pour the glue and 2½ Tbsps water into a large bowl. Gently stir until the two are thoroughly mixed together. Scrape the sides as needed.

2. Add the mini beads and stir until they are thoroughly mixed in. Add 3 drops blue food coloring. Mix in color completely.

3. Shake the starch well before you measure it out. Add a small amount of the liquid starch to the glue mixture and gently stir. The mixture will start to thicken and form slime. Keep stirring until the starch is well combined into the glue mixture.

4. Add a bit more liquid starch and stir very well. You may or may not need to add more starch. Add just enough to bring the slime into a soft lump or a ball. Adding too much of the starch will cause the slime to get very firm and not slime-like.

5. Knead the slime with both hands in the bowl for a bit. Place it on the table and knead some more. Continue kneading until the slime is stretchy and no longer sticky.

6. Clean-up is easy; just wash the spatula, bowl, measuring spoon, and measuring cup with hot soapy water. Store the slime for about a week in an airtight container.

23

Copyright © 2017 by Leisure Arts, Inc., 104 Champs Blvd., STE 100, Maumelle, AR 72113-6738, www.leisurearts.com. All rights reserved. This publication is protected under federal copyright laws. Reproduction or distribution of this publication or any other Leisure Arts publication, including publications which are out of print, is prohibited unless specifically authorized. This includes, but is not limited to, any form of reproduction or distribution on or through the Internet, including posting, scanning, or e-mail transmission.

We have made every effort to ensure that these instructions are accurate and complete. We cannot, however, be responsible for human error, typographical mistakes, or variations in individual work.

Production Team: Technical Writer – Mary Sullivan Hutcheson; Technical Associate – Jean Lewis; Editorial Writer – Susan Frantz Wiles; Senior Graphic Artist – Lora Puls; Graphic Artists – Marcus Boyce and Kellie McAnulty; Photostylist – Lori Wenger; Photographer – Jason Masters.